THE COMPLETE
GNOME MART CATALOGUE

Published in Great Britain
by Private Eye Productions Ltd,
6 Carlisle Street, London W1V 5RG,
in association with Corgi Books
Reprinted 1990

Designed by Bridget Tisdall
Photo-montage by Michael Bennett
Illustrated by
Gary Andrews, Barry Glynn,
Barry Fantoni and John Kent

Printed in Great Britain by
The Bath Press, Avon

Corgi Books are published by Transworld Publishers Ltd,
61-63 Uxbridge Road, Ealing, London W5 5SA,
in Australia by Transworld Publishers (Australia) Pty, Ltd,
15-23 Helles Avenue, Moorebank, NSW 2170
and in New Zealand by Transworld Publishers (N.Z.) Ltd,
Cnr. Moselle and Waipareira Avenues, Henderson, Auckland

THE COMPLETE GNOME MART CATALOGUE

PRIVATE EYE • CORGI

Do you remember last winter?
Don't be caught in the dark!

**YOU'LL NEVER
GET LOST
IN THE
DARK
AGAIN!**

thanks to these
SUPER NEW CANADIAN "WELLYLITE" ELECTRIC RUBBER BOOTS
Powered by own battery! Light your way as you walk!
Fully guaranteed for THREE MONTHS!!!
Send only £1 now and nine months payments of £3.65

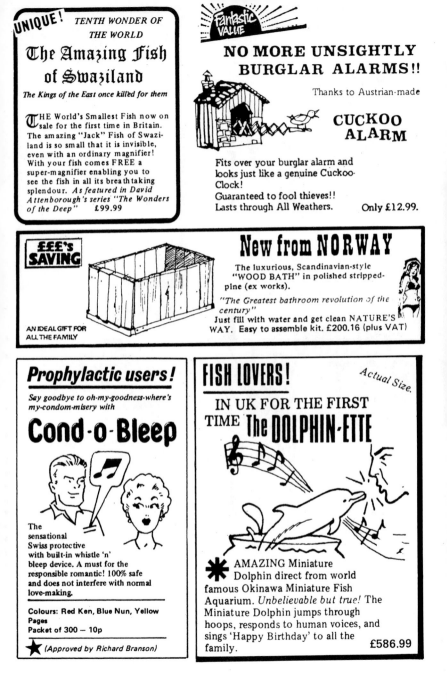

No more queuing for cash thanks to the new

Gnome Home Service Till

You will be the envy of your friends as they queue up for the cash point in the High Street on Saturday mornings. With your own Gnome Home ServiceTill, you merely go out of your front door and there it is on the wall of your home! Just insert your card and, bingo, cash is here!

Loadsamoney is yours! (Credit limit: £2,000.)

Fitted by our expert contractors, no fuss, easy to install.

Five-year waiting list.

Plays theme from Radio 4's popular *Moneybox* programme

£6,412,201

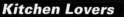

Bathroom novelty of the century!

Charles & Di Tap Tops

Beautify your washroom with these Right-Royal Taps. They're great. Charles is Hot — and Di's Cold (or whichever way you prefer). Just peel off, stick on top of the tap and hey presto — your bathroom looks like Buckingham Palace.

Fits all known sizes of tap. £47.99 per set

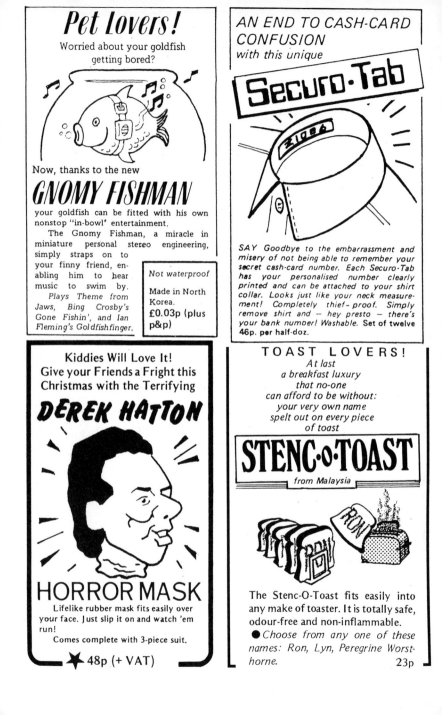

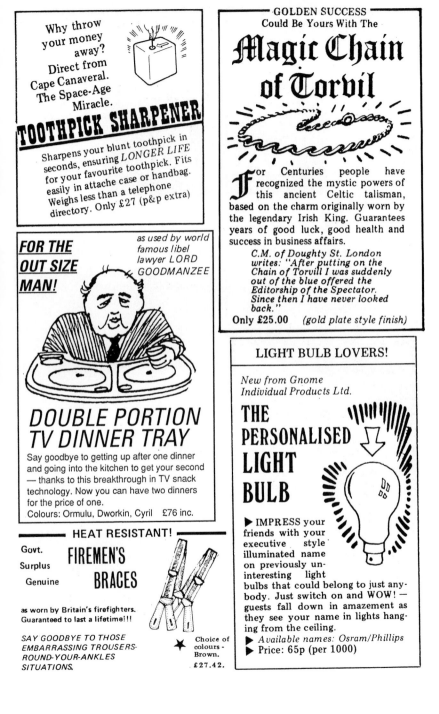

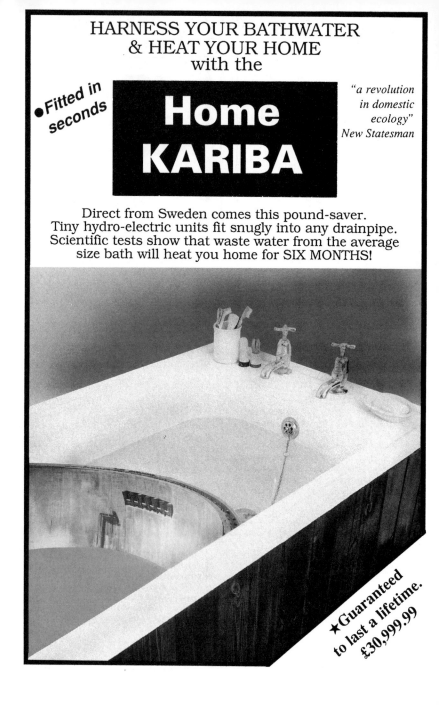

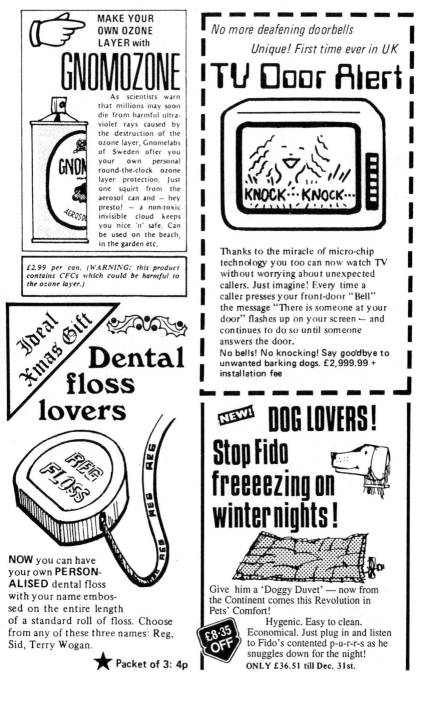

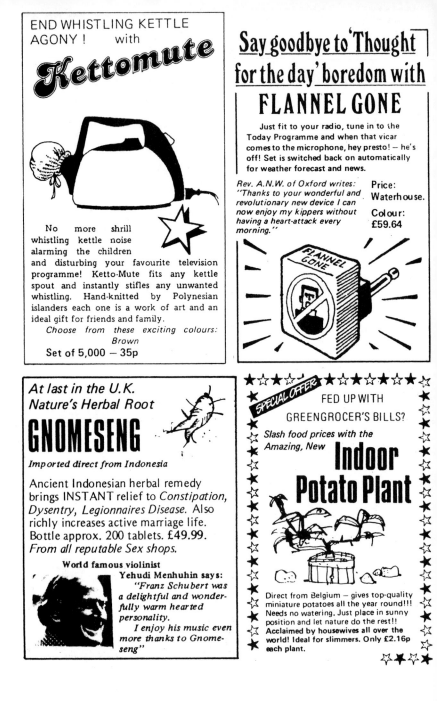

SAVE £££'s ON THOSE ELECTRICITY BILLS!

Wonder New Cook'N View

BAR·BE·TEL

brings into your home the world's first-ever Charcoal-Fired TV Set. No wires, no plugs! Just "Light up" two hours before you want to watch, and that TV-Dinner cooks while you view. It's incredible!

£4,819.52p (inc. VAT). Plus Free Bag of Charcoal with Every Order.

Get ready for the TV Explosion of the 1990s with

DISH-O-BROL

The amazing Dish-o-Brol keeps your Satellite Dish nice 'n' dry in all weathers. Thanks to the development of hi-tech Polygnomothene (as used in the Sri Lankan Space Programme), the Dish-o-Brol allows perfect reception at all times. Easy to erect, impossible to remove. Comes in stylish Riviera design which will enhance the neighbourhood and increase the value of your property.

Only £2,412.99

Alan Sugar says: "This will be a must for all dish-owners of tomorrow."

This Christmas! Join the latest fashion craze that is sweeping the nation with

THE COMPLETE BIG BANG WARDROBE

Sit at home in shirtsleeves with red braces and loosely-knotted spotted tie. Stare at the TV screen and pretend you're losing a fortune! Everybody's doing it!!

★ *De Luxe version includes window-ledge OR loaded shotgun (state preference.)*

Shirt sizes: 15½

Special Offer
Send in ten "Complete Big Bang Wardrobe" box lids and receive a FREE BP share application form.

☞ £39.99

BEARD LOVERS!

Control your beard with the revolutionary new

Beaverdoom

Swiss formula. Is easy to use. Handy sachets dissolve instantly in water. Just dip in comb, apply to the beard and — hey presto — watch unwanted beard growth disappear. Gauranteed harmless

+ FREE SAMPLE HEALTH COMB specially impregnated.
Money back if not satisfied. **£12**

Say Goodbye to Microwave Embarrassment with

The Palace of Fish Combined Aquarium and Microwave System

New from Cambodia, this incredible marriage of micro-technology and marine aesthetics turns a dreary kitchen gadget into an underwater wonderland of tropical fish.

The video screen oven door is programmed to show unlimited views of the following fish as they swim before your eyes:

Madagascar Guppy;
Golden Lion Fish of Hungary;
Cap'n Birdseye's Individual Tuna Fingers.

£700,000

Plays theme from THE BANDUNG FILE

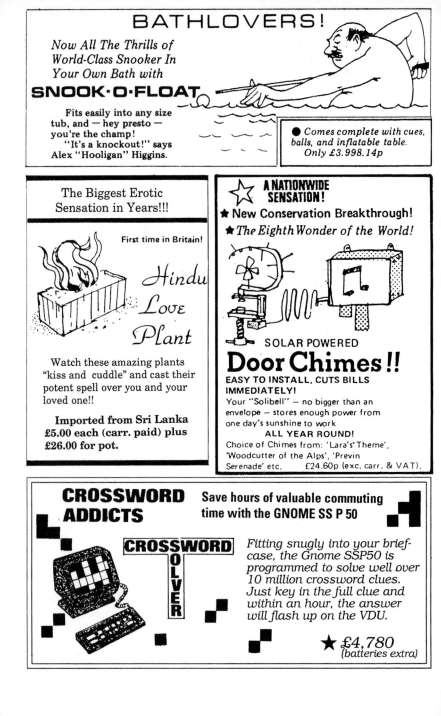

AMAZING!

FOR
KEEP FIT
FANS

VIDEO

HOME

JOGGER

Home jogging is no longer a chore thanks to this
fantastic new video experience! Running on the
spot is fun at last when this astonishing Video
Home Jogger opens up new vistas transporting
you to the running track of your choice. Moscow,
Montreal, Melbourne, Oslo — PLUS many more
of your favourites. Keep fit and see the world.

From £8,000 Seb Coe says *"When do I get my money!*

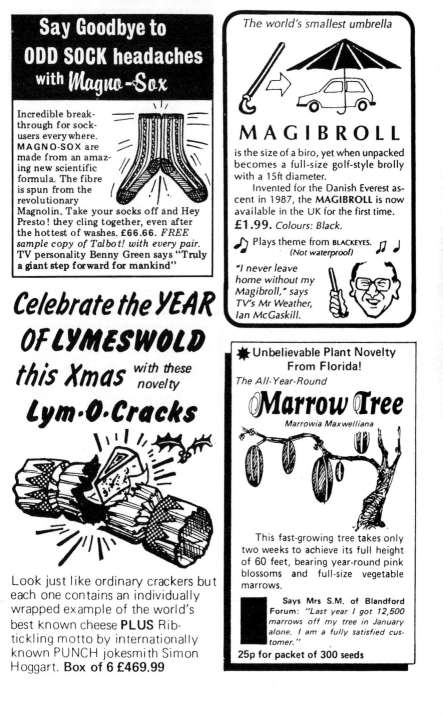

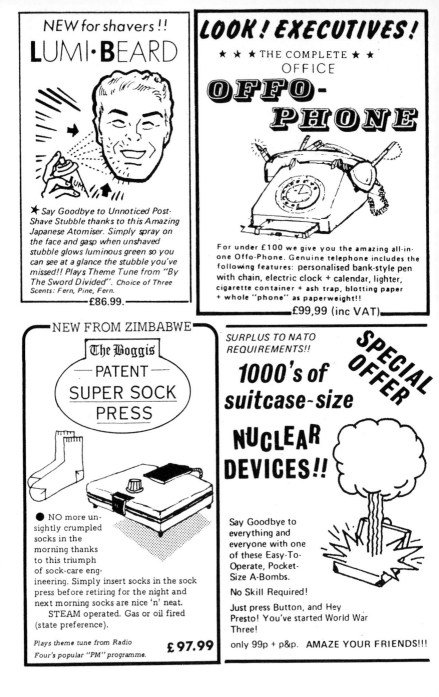

BARBECUE LOVERS!!

BARBE-GLOW
Artificial
Glow-worms

An end to not having any glow-worms in the garden when you're having a barbecue.

Identical in every way to the real thing and easier to catch!! Completely safe. Keep out of reach of children.

❦ **Set of 6 — £3.95** *(batteries extra)* ❦

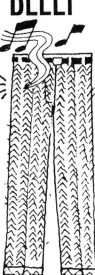

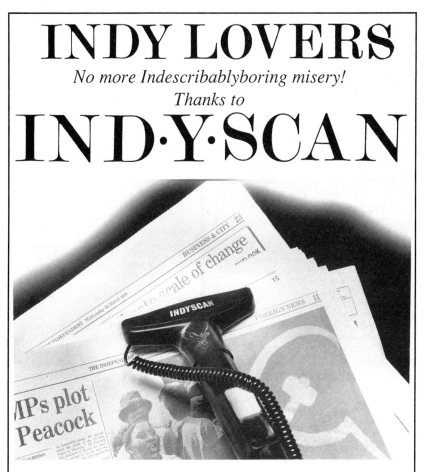

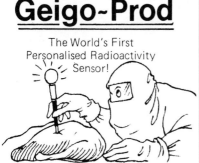

NOVEL-TREE!

FROM OCCIDENTAL AFRICA

THE AFRICAN JELLY PLANT

This tiny plant grows no bigger than a mushroom — yet it tastes just like Jelly. Unbelievable. Grows anywhere. £47.

AS ADVERTISED ON T.V.

1001 USES !!!

Be the Envy of Your Friends, at home or at the office with these Swedish-style

Magnetic CUFFLINKS

In chrome or gold-type finish, your "Magneticuffs" will give you hours of pleasure!!

80p each, or £1.60 the pair.

BUSINESSMEN!

The Dicta-Broll

Don't waste time under your umbrella, just because it's wet! Now thanks to the revolutionary new Dictaphone device from Taiwan, you can dictate vital letters and memos into the special microphone in the handle. *Mini-cassette doesn't miss a thing.* **£88,041.99.**

MOTORISTS *Get rid of those Red Light Blues with a*

GREEN-GO

automatic traffic light manipulator

(new from Reykjavik)

Simply point GREEN-GO at that irritating red light, press remote control switch to activate high-frequency sonic wave and, in seconds, the red light turns green!

Saves hours of frustration and misery! Gets you home from the office in time for your favourite TV show!

Only £10,487 *(plus nuclear power pack).*

■ *WARNING: This product is illegal. The makers accept no responsibility for improper use.*

Sellotape
users

Desk-Top Novelty From Austria

Sellotape ~ Recorder

Every time you use the Sellotape dispenser it automatically plays one of your favourite tunes. Choose from any one of these top hits: *"Jewel in the Crown Theme"*.

£89.99.   Colours: **Beige, Fawn, Biscuit.**

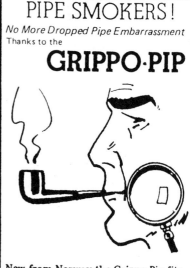

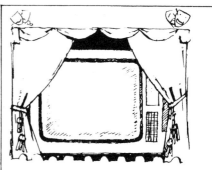

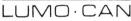

SAVE BUY FACTORY DIRECT

Say Goodbye to Bedtime Embarrassment with the **Denture Book Novelty**. This stylish looking 'Book' is really a handy container for your dentures. Fully waterproof. No one need ever know. Choose from these titles *War and Peace*, *Civilisation* by Lord Clark and *Mary Queen of Scots* by Lady Antonia Fraser.

A Gift to cherish.
Send £1.95 (incl.postage)

NEW!

SMOKERS

Revolutionary breakthrough in Tobaccology!

Introducing **AQUA-FAGS**

Say goodbye to "I can't have a smoke because I'm going underwater" misery! Now for the first time you can light up on the ocean floor. Whenever you feel like a puff, if you're scuba diving or if you've simply fallen off your windsurfer, just open a packet of "Aqua-Fags" then light up, and — hey presto! — lungs full of rich tobacco-flavoured smoke!

Packet of 20: £99
Underwater lighter extra (when invented)

**Jacques Cousteau says:
"J'adore les Aqua-Fags!"**

AMAZING!

BREAKTHROUGH IN IN-CAR-ENTERTAINMENT
Say goodbye to traffic jam misery with
this
WINDSCREEN VIDEO GAME

Turn your Windscreen into a Space Invaders Video Screen with this fantastic new invention from Gnome Leisure Productions. The Windscreen Video Game plugs easily into your dashboard Cigarette Lighter. Flick your indicator and Hey Presto! Unwanted Invaders Explode!!
£93,071.99. Choice of Games: *The Forces of Barg Varth*, *Doom warriors of Shiva* and *Creatures from the Black Stoddy*. (Thats enough games Ed.).

LAWN LOVERS!
Say goodbye to unkempt lawn misery with
☆ *Hawaian Screaming Grass*

Direct from South Korea

As soon as it grows above one inch in height this amazing grass lets out a piercing scream to let you know that its cutting time!! Just sit in your chair snug 'n' warm and wait for the screaming to begin.
Comes in handy ten-ton packets.
● *7p + p&p*

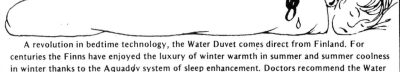

From the Pacific Hebrides!
THE AMAZING SPONGE of BALI

★ *Say Goodbye to bathroom hunger-blues*

THIS unique
bath sponge
can be actually
eaten — and is high
in minerals and protein!
Made from edible sea-weed
the Sponge of Bali is a must for
hungry bathers. Children love it.
State flavour: Marmite, Vanilla, Talbot etc.
£66.45 per pack of six

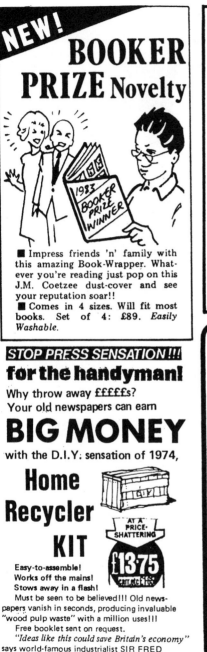

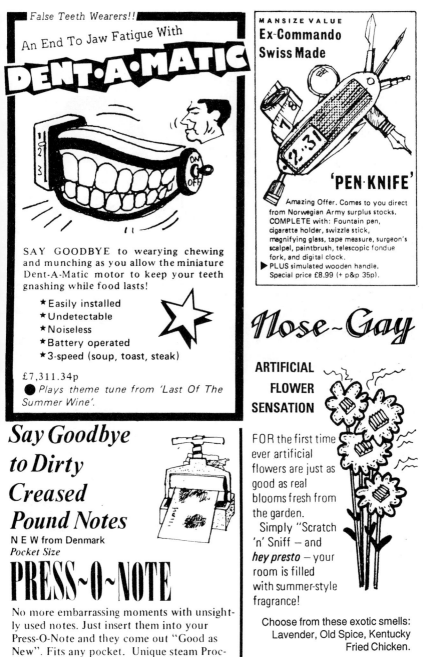

Filofax
Lovers

Introducing the

FILO-
FRIDGE

**Amazing miniature
fridge fits snugly into the back
of your Filofax. Ideal for cold drinks, snacks,
ice-cold coffee etc. The Filo-Fridge has a 5-star freezer
compartment, vegetable rack and ice-making facility.**
Battery powered. Plays theme tune from "First Among Equals"

£970.99

Say Goodbye to Germ-laden house flies

Battle of Britain Mobile Fly Killer

NOVELTY THAT FITS ANY ROOM!

Beautifully modelled Spitfire replicas coated with powerful insecticide bring instant death to German-looking flies + decorates your home all in one.

LASTS FOR YEARS
£161+p&p

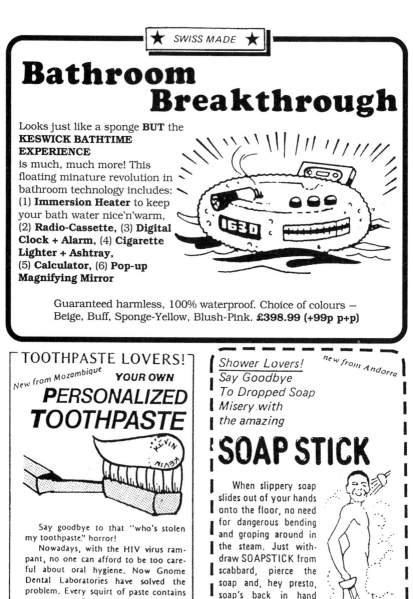

✳ **SAVE £££s** ✳
WITH THE LATEST ECO-MIRACLE FROM SWITZERLAND

THIS wind powered toaster turns nature's energy into piles of warm, crunchy toast without costing you a penny!

£ 412,64

(windmill extra)

Simply attach the 78 foot "windmill" to the side of your house, and, Hey Presto, toast's nice 'n' hot (subject to availability).

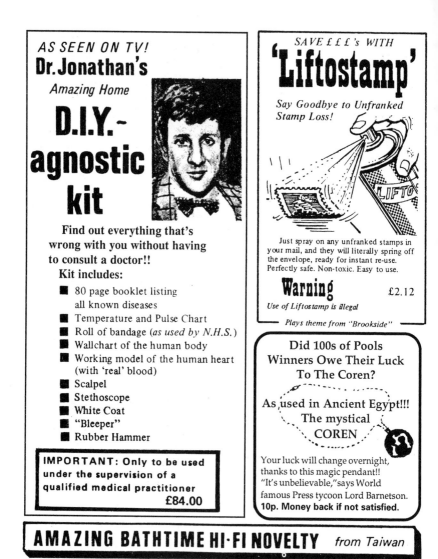

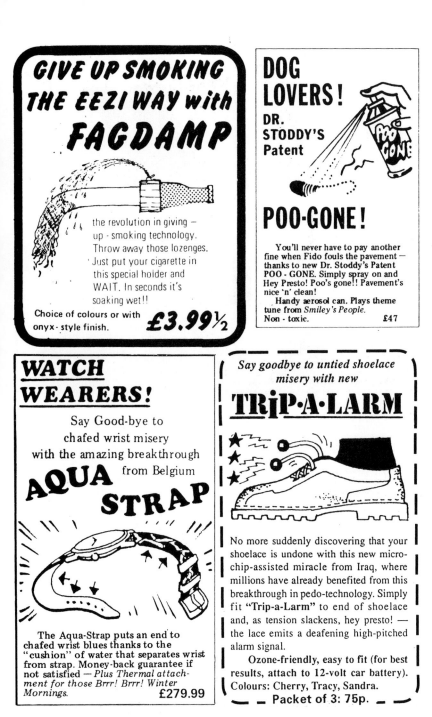

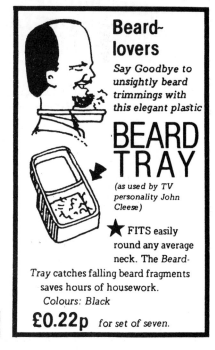

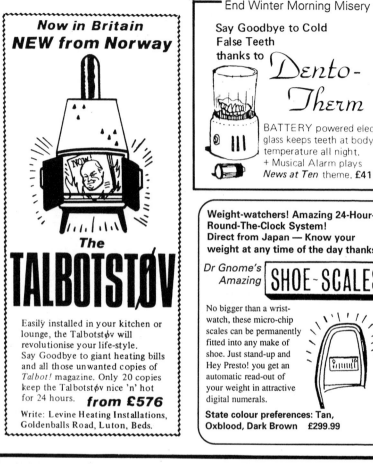

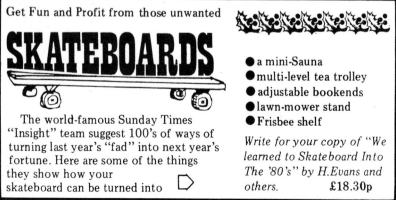

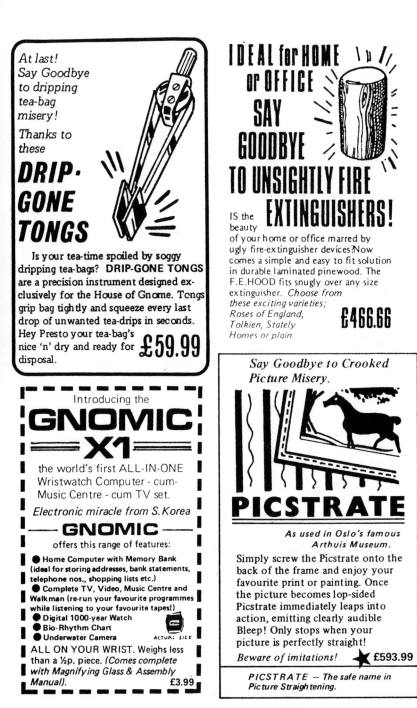

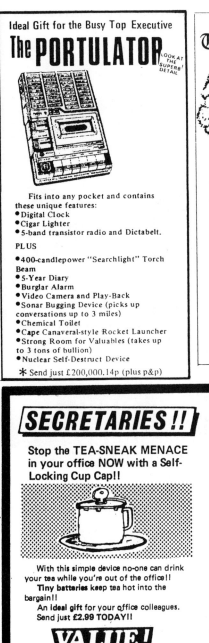

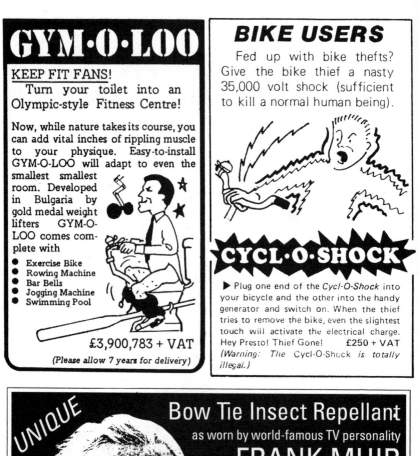

NEW FROM SHODDINGTON'S
— HOURS OF FUN
FOR ALL THE FAMILY

'BELGRANO'

(Pat. Pending)

Exciting, Real-Life War-Game for up to 16 Players. All the Thrill of the Falklands War and the Subsequent Cover-Up in your own living room.

Comes with Board, Log Book, and Dice.
£856.99